HARRIER Jump Jet

FRANK VANN

Brian Trodd Publishing House Limited

A Sea Harrier FRS 51 built by BAe prior to delivery to the Indian Navy.

Contents

The Development of the Jump Jet

Complicated aerobatics by skilled pilots never fail to hold the attention of any crowd of spectators. Sleek modern fighters crossing the sky at high speed are sure to thrill anyone who has been bewitched by the modern magic of flight. But the real show-stopper at any display in which it appears is the Harrier.

It can match most modern military aircraft for speed and surpass them in manoeuvrability, but its main claim to fame for the ordinary public is that it is the only fixed-wing aircraft which takes off vertically from the ground. It is a very impressive spectacle when, with a mighty roar from its engine, the Harrier lifts slowly and steadily into the air in front of the watching crowd.

Even more impressive is its ability to fly slower and slower until it comes to a complete stop in mid-air. The Harrier appears to be defying the laws of gravity as it reduces its speed until it hangs motionless in the sky. We are all used to associating the ability to stay in the air with the necessity to keep up a good forward speed. As a result, when the Harrier slows down, it is difficult to believe that the aircraft is not just about to stall and fall out of the sky. The Harrier can even fly backwards very sedately without losing altitude. Then, with another sudden roar from its engine it shoots up vertically and forwards like the agile combat aircraft which it really is.

How did this remarkable aircraft come to be designed and built?

How is it able to fly in a way in which no other aircraft can fly?

Left: A Harrier flying
easily in formation
with helicopters of the
"Blue Eagles" display
team at the Hawker
Aircraft Co. airfield at
Dunsfold in June 1975.
This is something most
other modern jet
fighters would find
hard to do.

Opposite: The
spectators at air
displays always gasp
in astonishment when
the Harrier performs
one of the vertical
take-off manoeuvres
shown here. The
aircraft climbs almost
vertically away from
the ground sustained
by the thrust from its
single engine.

What useful purpose can it serve in the armed forces of the free world?

This book is intended to answer all these questions and to give a better appreciation of the origins of this unique aircraft which today is in service with the Royal Air Force, the Royal Navy, the US Marine Corps, the Indian Navy and the Spanish Navy.

In order to keep an aircraft in the air it is necessary to generate an upward force at least as big as its weight. In airships this force is provided by a volume of gas which is lighter than air. In the case of the helicopter, an oversize propeller produces enough lift to support the weight of the aircraft. In conventional aircraft this force is produced by the air which flows over the wings. Because the cross-section of the wing is specially shaped, the air on the top of the wing has to move faster than the air below the wing. This produces a reduction of pressure on the top surface and a large upward load on the wing, and holds the aircraft up.

The difficulty with fixed wings is that they only generate a lift equal to the weight of the aircraft when they are moving through the air at high speed. Most modern jet-propelled aircraft have to have a forward speed of at least 195km/h (120mph) before the wings can lift them into the air.

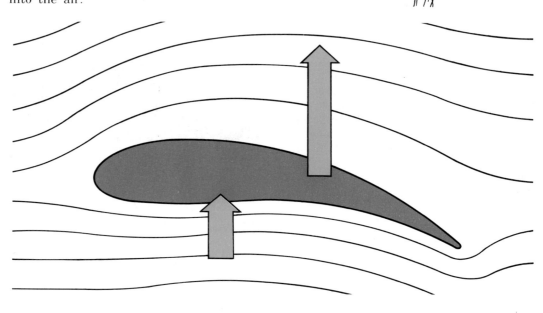

In order to reach this velocity, the aircraft has to take off by accelerating along the ground until it reaches the required take-off speed. This necessitates a long runway. A length of 2,000m (6,500ft) is not unusual for the runways on a civil airport. It takes almost that length of take-off run to get the aircraft off the ground. Runways do not need to be quite as long as that for the landing because modern brakes and the use of reverse thrust, or even braking parachutes on military aircraft, stop the aircraft in comparatively short distances.

The need for long runways is a decided disadvantage for military aircraft. Under wartime conditions, one of the first intentions of the enemy will be to destroy or badly damage runways so that aircraft are unable to be launched for the purposes of ground reconnaissance or for a counter-attack during a battle. All air forces today have specially designed bombs which penetrate the concrete of the runway before exploding. These produce very large holes in the surface of the runway and the perimeter tracks on which the aircraft travel to the take-off point, preventing conventional aircraft from taxiing or taking off. The damage can be repaired given sufficient time, but time is not usually available during a battle, especially one fought with modern weapons.

There was, therefore, a need for an aircraft which was not dependent on runways for its operations. The helicopter filled this role but, as of today, the speed of helicopters is restricted by the design of their lifting system based on rotors. Moreover, no helicopters can provide the manoeuvrability required to engage an incoming force of enemy aircraft.

What was needed was an aircraft capable of taking off from any unprepared

Here we see a Harrier concealed under a camouflage net in wooded country. It would be very difficult for an enemy to identify Harriers concealed in this way. A nearby road would enable the Harrier to take off and attack the opposing forces.

site and of flying fast enough to be useful in combat. This requirement had been recognized for many years before the Harrier was finally developed into an effective weapon.

If fixed wings required a long concrete runway, which might not be available in time of war, and if helicopters were too slow, what method of producing lift could be invented to overcome these problems?

This problem was taxing the imagina-

tions of aircraft designers in different countries in the 1950s. As is often the case, they were all coming up with similar ideas for a solution. They realized that the engine' thrust could in some way be arranged to act downwards. If the engine was powerful enough to produce more thrust than the weight of the aircraft, an aircraft could be lifted straight into the air from the ground. The engine thrust could be produced by a propeller or directly by a

jet engine. In fact, helicopters were already doing this but had the disadvantages mentioned earlier.

The first attempts at vertical take-off and landing (VTOL) were made with propeller-driven aircraft in the 1950s. Two early types produced as experimental aircraft in the United States were the Convair XFY-1 and the Lockheed XFV-1. Both of these aircraft stood upright on their tails before take-off. Large contra-rotating propellers driven by an Allison T40-A-14 engine provided the power. The aircraft were designed to take off vertically and then to turn over into the horizontal position so that their wings could sustain them for continued flight. Both of the aircraft performed successfully in flight trials but the idea was not pursued any further at the time.

In both the cases mentioned above, the thrust line was fixed relative to the aircraft. The transition from vertical to horizontal flight was achieved by tipping the whole aircraft over. Other designs soon followed in which the engines and the propellers could be swivelled relative to the aircraft. That meant that the aircraft could be kept horizontal while it changed from vertical to horizontal flight.

During this time, in England, the Rolls-Royce company were carrying out experiments into the possibility of vertical take-off and landing with jet engines using a trial installation which was soon given the irreverant name of the "Flying Bedstead". It was a simple frame, looking rather like a bedstead, in which were mounted two jet engines. The jet efflux from these engines pointed downwards to provide an upward thrust to lift the frame off the ground.

It had already been realized that control of the aircraft's attitude during the take-off would present some difficulties. Conventional control surfaces such as ailerons or rudders would not work until the aircraft had enough forward speed to provide airflow over them. They would certainly be almost useless during the transition from vertical to horizontal flight when the forward speed was very low.

On the "Flying Bedstead" air was tapped from the engine compressors and conducted through long tubes to downward-pointing nozzles on out-riggers sticking out of the sides of the frame. Because the nozzles were a long way from the centre of gravity of the craft, the reactions from these mini-jets provided the momentum to manoeuvre the frame while it was hovering. This was very far from being a true aircraft but the experience gained with the "Flying Bedstead" showed that jet engines could be used to achieve vertical take-off. It also demonstrated that aircraft could be safely controlled during the take-off phase by the use of jets acting vertically at the wing tips or at the front and rear ends of the fuselage.

The next move was obviously to design and build a complete aircraft including all the principles proved on the "Flying Bed-

The Lockheed XFV-1 is seen prepared for take-off. The contra-rotating propellers provide enough thrust to lift the aircraft vertically off the ground. Landing was extremely difficult since the pilot had to look back over his shoulder.

The engines were usually mounted on the wing tips. They initially stood vertically for take-off and then tilted forward to provide the thrust necessary for level flight. This made it easier for the pilot, who could sit upright relative to the ground during the whole manoeuvre. But it did not make it easy to feed the fuel to the engines or to run the engine controls to an engine whose position was changing.

This photograph explains clearly why the Rolls-Royce experimental aircraft was called the "Flying Bedstead". The outriggers carry at their ends the vertical jets which control the attitude in hovering flight.

stead". This aircraft appeared in the late 1950s in the form of the Short SC1. In that aircraft there were five engines. Four of them pointed downwards and provided the thrust needed to lift the aircraft off the ground. The fifth engine propelled the SC1 forward in flight in the normal way. Tests with the aircraft were successful and transition from hovering to forward flight was achieved without any major problems.

Although this was a good way of getting aircraft off the ground and into the air, it was not the best way of continuing to fly once the aircraft was airborne. Similar ideas were being discussed for commercial airliners but it was soon realized that this method of producing lift for continued flight by lifting jet engines was very uneconomical in the use of fuel. It was far more efficient to generate lift by a conventional set of wings once the aircraft was in the air over its take-off point. The best overall solution would be, therefore, firstly to lift the aircraft off the ground by direct thrust from its engines. Once it was airborne, the pilot would have to make a transitional manoeuvre by increasing the

13

The engine air intakes for the Short SC1 were on the upper side of the fuselage. This did not prevent them from becoming clogged by grass cuttings when the aircraft took off from a newly mown field.

forward speed of the aircraft until the wings produced enough lift to keep the aircraft flying in the same way as all other winged aircraft. At the same time he would reduce the vertical thrust from the engines to keep the aircraft in balance. This transitional manoeuvre looked as if it were going to need some new skills from the pilot.

The tests with the Short SC1 had also revealed some of the problems associated with VTOL. The downward blast from the lifting engines caused damage to the surface from which the aircraft operated. Even concrete soon began to break up under the blast effect from the jets. Debris stirred up from the ground was likely to be thrown into the air and ingested by the engine intakes, causing damage in the process. In one famous incident, the SC1 lifted off from a newly mown field. The grass cuttings swirled around and above the engines where they were sucked into the intakes. The layer of grass which built up on the intake grills completely blocked them, causing the engines to shut down.

A series of six photographs taken during early tests in which the Short SC1 carries out a vertical take-off (top row) and then a transition to forward flight (bottom row).

15

Like the SC1, the French Dassault "Balzac" used separate lift engines, eight in this case, to achieve VTOL in addition to its horizontal thrust engine for conventional flight.

Apart from damage due to the ingestion of debris from the ground, the hot exhaust gases from the lifting engines bounced back off the surface of the take-off area and were sucked back into the engine intakes. Jet engines prefer to operate by ingesting cool air. They do not work well when they are sucking in hot air contaminated with exhaust gases and are likely to demonstrate their displeasure by ceasing to provide as much thrust as they should. This is what happened during the tests with the SC1.

Altogether, a lot was learnt from the tests with the Short SC1. Like its predecessor, the "Flying Bedstead", it had demonstrated the possibility of vertical take-off and landing in principle. What

was now needed was a designer with the imagination and flair required to turn the ideas into a practical operational aircraft.

The next and most important part of the story was that written by the aircraft manufacturers, Hawker Aircraft Limited, in Kingston-upon-Thames on the outskirts of London. Hawker had long been famous as the designers and constructors of a series of very successful fighter aircraft including the Hind, the Hart and, most famous of all, the Hurricane. The Hurricane had played the main part in defending Great Britain against the German Luftwaffe during the Battle of Britain.

In the late 1950s, Hawker were looking for the aircraft to succeed the Hunter, one of Britain's first and most successful jet fighters. Many of the nations in NATO were interested in VTOL aircraft at that time. In particular, the United States, Germany and France all had proposals for military aircraft which did not depend on a fixed concrete runway for their operation. All of these projects still relied on the use of separate engines for vertical take-off and level flight. Hawker realized that this was a very inefficient way of achieving the desired result. Once the vertical take-off was completed, the lifting engines became so much useless dead-weight in the aircraft until they were needed again for the landing. If one and the same engine could be used both to lift the aircraft off the ground and to propel it in the horizontal flight phase, the weight of the lift engines could be replaced by

The VJ 101 achieved vertical take-off by rotating its engines relative to the wing tip. This made it possible to alter the angle of the thrust line without changing the attitude of the fuselage. It obviously made the pilot's job much easier.

armaments and make the aircraft a much more effective fighting machine.

But was such an engine available? If so, how could its thrust be directed downwards for take-off and then backwards for flight? The answer to both these questions was provided by the Bristol Engine Company in 1957. They offered a developed version of the Bristol Orpheus engine which was equipped with rotating nozzles. If the nozzles pointed downwards, the engine thrust was used to lift the aircraft vertically. When the aircraft reached a suitable altitude, the nozzles could be rotated so that the jets pointed backwards and the thrust would drive the aircraft forwards.

This simple idea made possible a major step forward in the achievement of a practical aircraft whch would not be dependent on hard runways in wartime for its successful operation. It would be able to take off from a clearing in a wood or from any flat surface in a city or on a motorway. The enemy would find it difficult to locate large numbers of such aircraft dispersed over the countryside and would have to destroy each of the aircraft on the ground one at a time to prevent them from being used against him. That would be a very different proposition from grounding a large number of aircraft at once by dropping one bomb on their runway and preventing them from taking off.

Once the aircraft was safely in the air, it would be able to perform as well as any conventional fighter and could carry a

The Russians, too, build VTOL aircraft as is shown by this photograph of three Yak 38 Forgers. The aircraft are powered by three engines, two nose-mounted, dedicated lift engines and one lift/cruise engine with thrust vectoring. They are deployed aboard Soviet Kiev class carriers.

formidable array of offensive weapons, allowing it to attack a wide range of targets.

The first of this type of aircraft which Hawker designed was given the type number of P1127. It was not intended to enter service as an operational aircraft. Its purpose was to test in flight all the new ideas which it embodied and to discover any problems involved in the new technology. Once these problems had been identified, and suitable solutions found, it would be possible to design a vertical take-off aircraft which would perform in service in a way that no aircraft had ever been able to perform before.

The first success achieved with the P1127 was the transition from vertical to horizontal flight. The "Flying Bedstead" had been equipped with auto-stabilizers. These took over from the pilot the task of keeping the aircraft on an even keel. If the auto-stabilization system detected a tendency of the aircraft to deviate from the horizontal position, it automatically admitted air to one of the nozzles on the outriggers and corrected the attitude of the aircraft. Although this system worked well on an experimental rig such as the "Flying Bedstead", it would place restrictions on the pilot when he wanted to control the attitude of an aircraft in combat. The auto-stabilizer might have different ideas from the pilot on the best way of manoeuvring the aircraft. For this reason, Hawker decided to design a control system which was entirely under the pilot's control.

The development of the Harrier was not without certain problems. This picture shows a P1127 which crashed while on display at the 1963 Paris Air Show.

These two diagrams illustrate the engine's nozzle position, thrust lines, and the aircraft's direction of motion during a vertical take-off and transition to forward flight (right) and for a short rolling take-off (below).

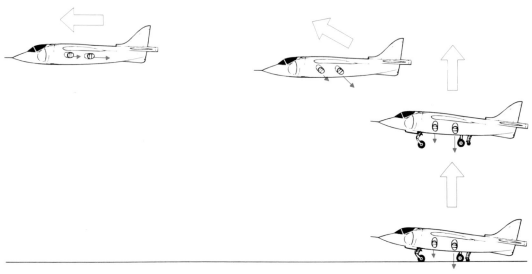

In fact, early trials with the P1127 showed that the difficulties which it had been feared would occur during the transition from vertical to horizontal flight simply did not happen. When the aircraft was hovering above the ground after a vertical take-off, the jet nozzles could be rotated slowly backwards. This produced a forward force which made the aircraft slowly accelerate into normal flight. At the same time the vertical component of the lifting force reduced until, when the nozzles were horizontal, there was no lift from the jets. The secret lay in adjusting the speed of rotation of the nozzles so that the increase of lift on the wings (as the aircraft moved forward) exactly balanced the loss of lift from the jets. In this way, the aircraft accelerated forward in level flight without losing height as it did so.

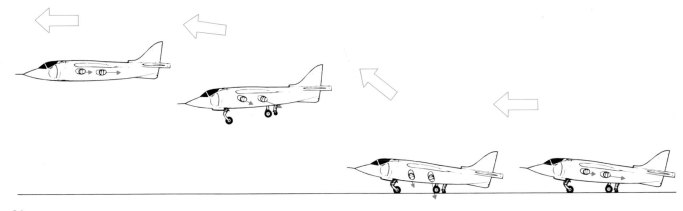

The second problem that was solved with the P1127 was the "short take-off". Because of the limitation of the thrust provided by the early engines, the amount of payload which the aircraft was able to carry was limited. It was realized that if the P1127 could taxi forward like a conventional aircraft, the wings could generate lift before take-off in the same way as any other aircraft. This lift could be added to the vertical thrust from the jets and enable a larger payload to be lifted. The take-off would no longer be vertical but it would be much steeper than any other aircraft could achieve.

Trials started in 1961 to perfect the procedures necessary. In this case, the pilot started off with the nozzles tilted backwards to accelerate the aircraft for-wards and build up lift on the wings. When the correct speed was reached, the nozzles were directed downwards to provide lift and the aircraft was raised into the air. The nozzles were then rotated back again in the same way as after a vertical take-off. This manoeuvre was successfully achieved for the first time in October 1961.

It was not long before it was realized that the P1127 would be ideal for operation from an aircraft carrier, or indeed, from much smaller ships. Fighter aircraft had been flown from ships since World War I. However, in the early days they had had to be catapult-launched and were unable to land back on to the ship at the end of their mission. When the use of aircraft in sea operations became an

Above: The P1127 was still engaged in trial operations from a carrier ship when this photograph was taken in 1964.

Right: Two P1127 test aircraft are seen in flight during the experimental evaluations carried out by the tripartite trials team, from the UK, the US and West Germany.

accepted principle, aircraft carriers were designed whose decks formed runways from which aircraft could take off with the help of steam catapults. The decks were also long enough to allow aircraft to land back on to the carrier. Aircraft carriers by reason of their extremely large size were very vulnerable to attack by enemy forces. With an aircraft like the P1127, any ship however small could become an aircraft carrier if it had an area of a few square yards to use as a take-off and landing platform.

The first take-offs and landings on a carrier were successfully completed in February 1963. It was found that it was no more difficult to operate from a carrier than from a fixed land site. By this time, all of the major problems associated with VTOL operation had been investigated. None of them had proved insuperable and it was obvious that a military aircraft could be built which could operate from a

very small site without the need for a long runway. Many transitions from vertical take-off to horizontal flight and back again had been successfully carried out. More powerful engines were becoming available so that bigger military payloads could be carried over greater distances.

The British government showed its faith in the new type of aircraft by placing an order for an improved version of the P1127 in 1962 which was given the name of "Kestrel". These aircraft were introduced into the Royal Air Force and pilots began to accumulate experience in the handling of what to them was a completely new type of flying machine. Trials with the Kestrel continued until late 1965. At the end of that year, six Kestrels were sent to the United States for evaluation by the US Air Force.

In 1966, major improving modifications were introduced into the aircraft as a result of the large amount of experience which had been gained. The basic layout remained unaltered but the structure was extensively altered to allow for higher weights, more powerful engines and the carriage of a wider variety of armaments. The new aircraft was given the name "Harrier" and 60 were ordered for the

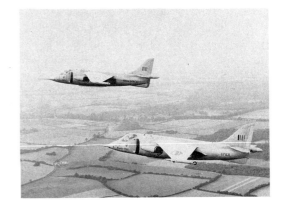

Left: An early
demonstration of in-
flight refuelling of the
Harrier from a Victor
tanker. Refuelling
operations of this type
allowed the Harrier to
compete in the
Transatlantic Air Race
of 1969.

Below: The early ski-
jump tests to prove the
practicality of that
means of shortening
the take-off distance
were carried out on a
platform built for
British Aerospace by
Fairey Engineering
Ltd. Here BAe's
Harrier T.2 is seen
powering its way up
the ramp.

Royal Air Force. After years of doubt, uncertainty and rejection by military experts who should have known better, the Harrier was about to embark on a brilliant career which was to reach its climax in the campaign to liberate the Falkland Islands after their invasion by Argentina in 1982.

A further development helped to assist the operation of Harriers from aircraft carriers. In 1972, it was realized that the distance required by the Harrier for a "short take-off" could be reduced if it ran forward on to a sloping surface which would force it up into the air. The first trials with the so-called "ski jump" were carried out in 1977. They proved so successful that this idea has been incorporated into all carriers which operate Harriers.

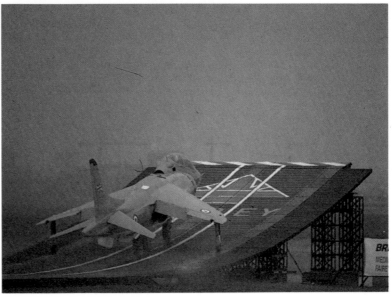

The anhedral of the Harrier wing is clearly visible in this head-on view. It also illustrates the arrangement of the undercarriage with the main wheels on the centre-line of the aircraft and stabilizing wheels mounted on outriggers near the wing tips.

Today, the Harrier is in service with the Royal Air Force, the Royal Navy, the US Marine Corps, the Indian Navy and the Spanish Navy in a number of different versions. The main difference between the various types are the engine power, the instrumentation and the armaments carried. The three main versions of the Harrier are described later, but following are the features which are common to all the variants.

The Harrier is not a large aircraft. Its wing span is just over 7.6m (25ft) in the earlier versions. This has been extended to slightly more than 9m (30ft) on the Harrier II and the AV-8B. The wing is highly tapered and the leading edge is swept back sharply. When looked at from the front the wing is distinguished by the noticeable anhedral. That means that, instead of being flat, the wing slopes down towards the tips.

Pylons are fitted to "hard points" beneath the wings to carry external stores, such as bombs, unguided rockets, long-range fuel tanks or guided missiles. Sidewinder, air-to-air, infra-red homing missiles can be carried on launching rails mounted on the outermost pylons.

The wing itself is made in one piece extending from tip to tip. It has been designed to withstand flight accelerations of $+7.8g$ to $-4.2g$.

The Harrier has an unconventional undercarriage. The main wheels are all located on the centre-line of the aircraft so that the main undercarriage is something like a bicycle. To prevent the aircraft from toppling over sideways on the ground, small wheels are mounted on outriggers under the outer wings. The loads due to the contact of the small wheels on the ground provide the design loads for parts of the wing structure.

The inner part of the wings forms a fuel tank. This part of the wing has three spars running along its length. Outboard of the fuel tank there are only two spars. The top and bottom wing skins on the early Harriers are machined from thick aluminium alloy plate which is tapered along the span to suit the local load levels. Designing a wing with the minimum weight is important for any aircraft and this is particularly true for the Harrier. Every pound saved in the structure can be used for an extra pound of armaments.

Outboard of the main wing structural box it is possible to fit either a standard wing tip or a larger tip used to give extra lift for long distance ferrying of the aircraft. The bigger tip gives extended range but reduces the manoeuvrability of the aircraft. It is, therefore, not suitable for use in combat where the ability to perform tight manoeuvres can mean the difference between life and death.

The Harrier wing is equipped with the normal type of ailerons and flaps similar to most other aircraft. On the early Harriers these were of conventional aluminium construction. The later developed

Above: Although the AV8B Harrier is not a large aircraft, it can carry a selection from the awesome array of armaments shown here.

Left: The geometry of the Harrier landing gear can be clearly seen from this view taken shortly after take-off.

versions have these surfaces made of
carbon fibre composite materials. The
wing tips on later aircraft are also carbon
fibre.

Like the wing, the tailplane has a
noticeable amount of anhedral. On the
early Harriers, the construction was of
high-strength aluminium alloy. Later versions, including the American built AV-
8B, now have the tail surfaces made of
carbon-fibre-reinforced composite material. The two sides of the tailplane are built
as one unit, tip to tip, in the same way as
the wings. The thicknesses of the top and
bottom skins are again tapered like those
on the wing so that the more lightly
loaded sections near the tip are thinner
and lighter.

Because the Harrier often has to operate at high speed very close to the ground,
it is in danger from bird impact. Although
most birds are very light, the damage
caused by striking a bird at over 965km/h
(600mph) can be very severe. Even a

small bird weighing only half a kilogram
(1lb) can punch a hole in a sheet of metal.
In fact, it can cause the loss of the
unfortunate aircraft and its crew. For this
reason, the leading edge of the wing has to
be made strong to resist the impact of a
bird. On the Harrier, the leading edge is
3.2mm thick so that the bird will not
penetrate the skin and puncture the fuel
tank between the spars.

The pilot's windscreen has also been
designed to stand up to the impact of a
bird. In that case, not only must the bird
be unable to punch a hole in the windscreen: even it if fails to get through the
glass transparency, it must not cause
fragments of glass to fly off the inside of
the window into the face of the pilot.

The heart of the Harrier is obviously its
engine and the system of nozzles which
enable vertical take-off to be achieved.
The Harrier is powered by a Rolls-Royce
(Bristol) Pegasus engine. Over the years,
the engine has been continually developed
so that the latest versions can output a
thrust of more than 9,525kg (21,000lb).

All jet engines suck air into their forward intake and compress it by means of
an axial flow compressor. ("Axial flow"
means that the air travels in a direction
parallel to the axis of the engine as it
passes through. The first jet engines had
centrifugal compressors in which the air
was compressed by being thrown out-
wards from the axis of the engine.) Fuel is
then injected into the compressed air and
ignited. This produces a large amount of
hot exhaust gas at an even higher pressure. Some of the thrust from the engine is
produced by allowing the hot air to escape
from the jet-pipe at the rear of the engine.
On its way to the jet-pipe the hot air has
to pass through a turbine which is really
just a large fan which is blown round by

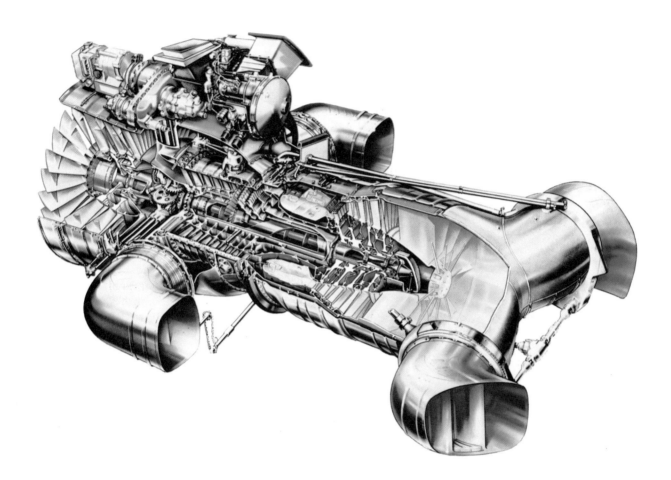

the escaping gases. The turbine is mounted on the same shaft as the compressor. By driving the compressor, the turbine provides the power to force more air into the intake. Once the engine has started, therefore, the whole cycle continues until the fuel is cut off.

Most modern jet engines are made more efficient by using them to power a large fan at the front end of the engine, in

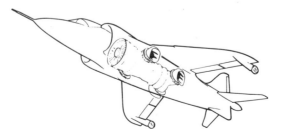

Left: This drawing shows the position of the Pegasus engine installation relative to the rest of the aircraft. The positioning of the nozzles ensures that the total engine lift is balanced about the centre of gravity.

addition to providing thrust directly from the exhaust jet. The fan is really another compressor but the air which it compresses does not flow through the centre of the engine. Instead it is diverted through a duct around the engine casing and produces thrust in the same way as an old-fashioned propeller.

The air which goes through the core of the engine is moving very fast and is very hot when it leaves the jet-pipe. The air which has passed through the fan is moving much more slowly and is cold. On a normal jet-engine the slow-moving cold air forms a kind of tube around the fast-moving hot air. They are both directed backwards and both contribute to the total thrust from the engine.

On the Harrier, things are arranged differently. The air issuing from the hot core of the engine and the air coming out of the fan are kept separate. In both cases, the air is directed into two nozzles, one on each side of the engine. These nozzles can be rotated so that they direct the jets in a direction parallel to the plane of symmetry of the aircraft. If the nozzles are pointing downwards, the thrust acts vertically upwards and lifts the aircraft. If they are turned so that the air rushes out backwards, the thrust will drive the aircraft forwards.

The operating mechanisms of the nozzles are connected together so that they all move in the same direction at the same time. The pilot has a control in the

The four nozzles are geared together so that they all point in the same direction. The mechanism is very simple and consists of a pneumatically driven actuator connected to the nozzles by chain and sprocket drives.

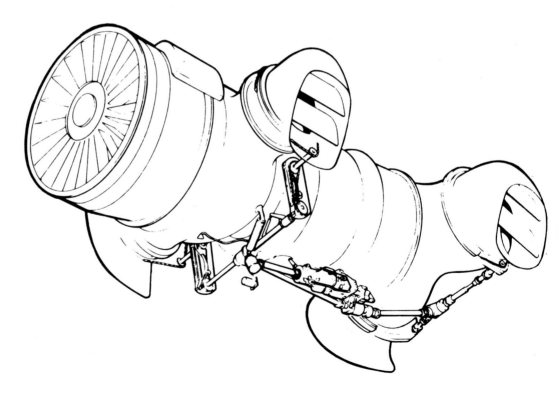

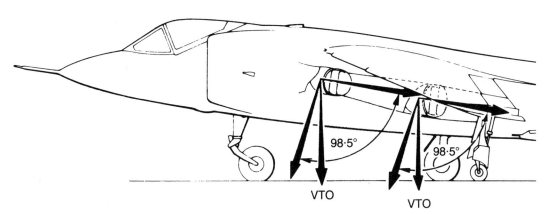

This diagram shows the range of engine nozzle movement. For take-off/landing and jetborne flight they are directed downwards, while in cruising/high speed flight the nozzles are rotated aft. Prior to landing, the aircraft is slowed by rotating the nozzles to their forward stops, thus directing the downward thrust slightly forward of the vertical and providing an effective brake.

98·5°   98·5°

VTO   VTO

cockpit which moves the nozzles by a mechanical system. This nozzle lever is the only additional control in the Harrier cockpit which is not already familiar to the pilot of a conventional aircraft. The four nozzles and the mechanism for rotating them divert the thrust in the required direction. This process is known as "thrust vectoring" which is just a mathematical way of saying that the direction of the thrust can be altered.

Mention has already been made of the difficulty to control the aircraft when it is hovering. Until air starts to flow over the control surfaces, they cannot produce any loads to alter the attitude of the aircraft. On the Harrier, air can be tapped off from the high pressure compressor of the engine and conducted to reaction nozzles at the extremities of the aircraft in the same way as on the "Flying Bedstead". There are vertical nozzles at the front and rear of the fuselage which can control the aircraft in pitch. Similar nozzles at the wing tips can control the aircraft in roll. At the rear of the fuselage is a nozzle pointing sideways which is used to swing the Harrier around sideways.

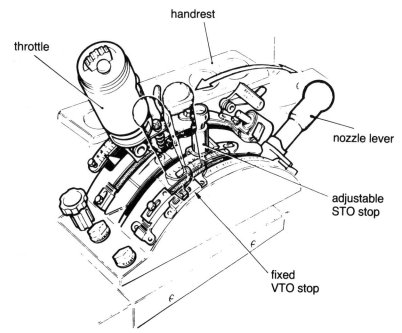

handrest

throttle

nozzle lever

adjustable STO stop

fixed VTO stop

The pilot's controls for the wing tip reaction jets are connected into the same system as the normal aileron controls. The pilot's actions are the same, therefore, during hovering as in conventional flight and he notices no difference in the

The only control unique to the Harrier is the nozzle lever. The aircraft will lift off vertically as the throttle is opened.

When flying in the conventional manner the Harrier is supported by the wing generated lift, and is controlled by the normal set of ailerons, elevators and a rudder.

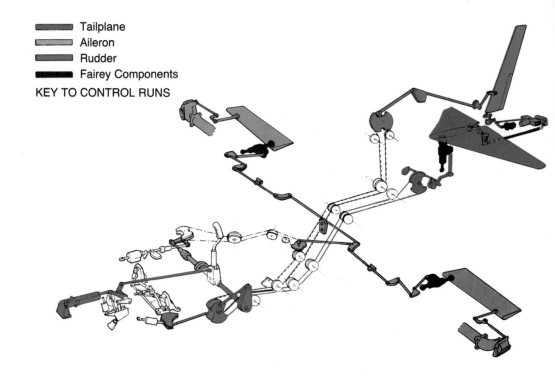

Tailplane
Aileron
Rudder
Fairey Components
KEY TO CONTROL RUNS

When the Harrier is hovering and supported by the engine jets alone, there is no airflow over the wings or tail surfaces. Conventional controls cannot then change the attitude of the aircraft. Instead, air is bled from the engine and piped to small nozzles at the wing tips and at the front and rear of the fuselage to enable the pilot to manoeuvre while hovering.

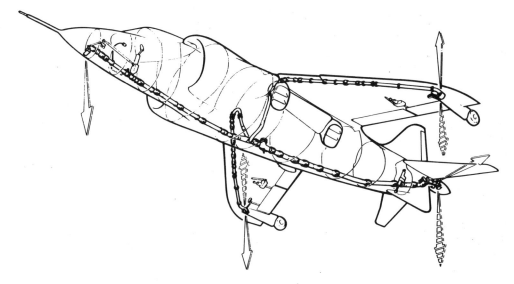

The small, freely hinged doors seen immediately behind the intake of this Harrier T.2 serve as pressure relief valves. By opening inwards they prevent the intake shoulder structure from collapsing when near maximum throttle is applied while the aircraft is at low speed or stationary. When a Harrier is parked, the doors on top of the intake fall open under their own weight and, similarly, those below close.

actions required of him during the transition from vertical take-off to forward flight.

As also mentioned earlier, one of the most difficult problems which had to be solved was the recirculation of hot gases from the engine jets back into the intakes. The effects could be reduced to a minimum by the correct design of the engine air intakes. These can be seen as the large semicircular bulges on each side of the fuselage beneath the cockpit. Unfortunately, the best shape of intake to prevent re-ingestion of hot exhaust air on the ground is not the same as the most efficient shape for high-speed flight. Some way of altering the shape of the lips of the intake was required. Early P1127s had inflatable flexible lips at the front edge of the intake. By pumping air into the lips, their shape could be altered to suit the flight conditions.

Early in the flight trials it was found that these flexible lips could not stand up to the big loads to which they were subjected during flight at high speeds close to the speed of sound. Some more robust solution to the problem had to be found.

All the Harriers now have small doors arranged around the front part of the intake cowlings. By altering the setting of the doors, the air flow into the intake can be controlled to suit the flight conditions. They also assist in keeping the re-ingestion of the exhaust gases to a minimum.

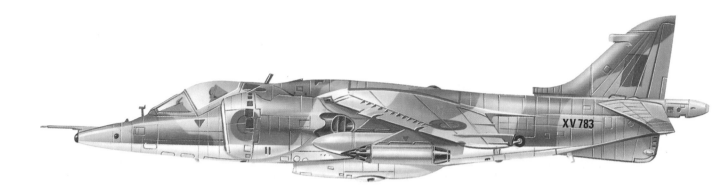

RAF Harriers

The Harriers in service with the Royal Air
Force are equipped with the Ferranti
Inertial Navigation and Attack System
(INAS). In simple terms, this enables the
pilot to know where he is and where the
enemy are relative to him. With the aid of
the INAS, he can find his targets and aim
his weapons very accurately.

During combat, the pilot cannot afford
to be continually looking down to read his
flight instruments. He has to keep his
eyes focused on his target. The Head-Up
Display (HUD), mounted on top of the
instrument console, projects the essential
flight information from the instruments
on to a transparent screen which is in the
pilot's line of vision. The readings appear
to him to be floating in the sky in front of
him. In this way, he can keep his eyes on
the target and read the information from
all the essential instruments at the same
time.

To assist him in navigating his aircraft,

the pilot is provided with all the most
up-to-date avionic systems. He can also
refer to a moving map display which is
projected on to a screen in the cockpit.
This shows him his exact position on the
map during the whole flight. A forward
facing infra-red searchlight allows him to
see as well by night as he can in daylight.

The RAF Harriers carry very sophisti-
cated equipment to make it easy for the
pilot to aim his weapons more quickly and
accurately. The official title of this equipment is Laser Ranging and Marked
Target Seeker Equipment. This identifies
and locates the target and measures the
range very accurately by the use of infra-
red radiation.

When he is attacking a target from a
very low altitude, it is essential for the
pilot to know if he has been picked up by
enemy radar.

The Harrier carries a Radar Warning
Receiver for that purpose. Air-to-air and
air-to-ground communications are provided by UHF/VHF (ultra high frequency

and very high frequency) radios.

To enable him to get out of the aircraft quickly in an emergency, the pilot can make use of a Martin Baker ejector seat. This is a rocket propelled seat which is fired upwards out of the cockpit with the pilot still seated in it.

When he finds it necessary to eject, the pilot pulls the firing handle. This action automatically secures the pilot's legs and body in the seat so that he does not injure his limbs as he is fired up through the cockpit canopy. At the top of the seat is a strong structure which breaks through the canopy to provide a way out for the seat and the pilot. When the seat is at a safe distance from the aircraft, a drogue parachute slows the seat down. The pilot's own parachute then opens and he is automatically separated from the seat before floating gently down to safety on the ground.

Above: The ejector seat operation is dramatically shown during trials with a mock-up nose and cockpit on a rocket-propelled sled at China Lake Naval Weapons Center, California.

Opposite: The RAF's latest Harrier: the GR5.

Sea Harriers

The Sea Harrier FRS Mk1 is a version of the Harrier designed to meet the special requirements of the Royal Navy. It is intended to operate at sea from aircraft carriers as a fighter, reconnaissance aircraft or in an offensive attack role.

These aircraft proved their worth during the Falklands campaign in 1982. Thirty-eight Sea Harriers were sent with the Royal Navy to the South Atlantic where there were no fixed bases from which British aircraft could operate. It would not be an exaggeration to say that they played the leading part in the success of that campaign and that, without them, victory would have been impossible.

This version of the Harrier is armed for the anti-ship role. It can launch the Sea Eagle air-to-surface missile which flies low over the sea until it homes-in on its target with devastating results.

British Aerospace is at present in the process of updating 29 of the Royal Navy's 42-strong Sea Harrier FRS 1 force to FRS 2 standard. The principal difference of the updated aircraft is a new Ferranti radar which will give the FRS 2 the ability to attack up to four airborne targets at once, using the newly developed Advanced Medium-Range Air-to-Air Missile, AIM-120 AMRAAM.

An export version of the Sea Harrier is also in service with the Indian Navy, and is known as the FRS 51.

Right: The Sea Harrier FRS Mk1 is a navalized version developed for use by the Royal Navy. The nearest aircraft is armed with four AIM-9L Sidewinders and two underbelly 30mm Aden gun pods; it is also equipped with two range-extending drop tanks. These aircraft proved their value during the Falklands campaign of 1982.

Opposite: Designed specifically to operate V/STOL aircraft, the Royal Navy operates three Invincible class carriers. Seen on the deck of HMS *Invincible*, shown here, are four Sea Harrier FRS Mk 1s, along with a Sea King helicopter. Just visible in this view is the "ski jump" toward the bow.

AV-8A and AV-8B Harrier II

From the start of the early Hawker trials with the P1127 aircraft, great interest was shown in the United States in these new developments. Indeed, American funding had kept alive the work on the Pegasus engine when the British government was showing little interest. The wind tunnel testing of the free-flight model of the P1127 had also been tested in the NASA Langley wind tunnels.

In 1962, it was proposed that Hawkers should try to find an American manufacturer who would develop the P1127 into a version suitable for use by the US Navy. The Northrop Corporation expressed an interest in 1963 and an agreement with them was signed by which an exchange of information between the two companies would take place. In the end, no aircraft were built in the USA but Northrop played a useful role in interesting influential people in US defence circles in the possibilities of VTOL aircraft.

In 1966, six Kestrels were shipped to the USA for evaluation by service pilots. The flight trials aroused great enthusiasm in the US Marine Corps, who could see a very useful application for VTOL aircraft in their planned activities.

By 1969, matters had progressed so far that a team of US Navy test pilots visited Great Britain to carry out flight trials to evaluate the merits of the Harrier. As a result, later that same year the US Marine Corps obtained the funding to buy 12 Harriers with the stated intention of buying 114 by the middle of 1970.

Part of the deal was an agreement that much of the actual building of the aircraft would be done in the USA. Before the end of 1969, Hawker Siddeley Aviation (into which Hawker had been absorbed in the meantime) signed a licensing agreement with McDonnell Douglas, a company with unmatched experience in the design and manufacture of military aircraft. Part of the agreement stated that the British company gave McDonnell Douglas the exclusive rights to the sale and manufacture of the Harrier and any derivatives in the USA for a period of 15 years.

The American version of the Harrier was given the designation AV-8A. In service with the US Marine Corps, the AV-8A fully justified all the expectations which had been associated with it. The aircraft fitted ideally into the type of operations which the Marines saw as their areas of future involvement. Instead of using large aircraft carriers, which were expensive and vulnerable to attack, the

Right: A US Marine Corps' AV-8A takes off from the flight deck of the US assault ship *Tripoli*.

An AV-8A of the US
Marine Corps in
hovering flight. The
forward nozzle can be
seen rotated to its
downward position to
produce the thrust
required to support the
aircraft.

Above: This air-to-air shot shows an early developmental version of the AV-8B, used to flight test the new carbon-fibre wing.

Opposite: The ability of Harriers to operate in the most severe weather conditions is demonstrated by this photograph of the snow-covered flight-deck of an assault ship of the "Tarawa" class. Two AV-8B Harriers make their way to their take-off positions past parked Boeing CH-46 Sea Knight helicopters.

same purpose could easily be served by a larger number of smaller ships carrying AV-8As.

The latest version of the Harrier, known as the AV-8B or the Harrier II, is being built in a joint enterprise by British Aerospace (who have now incorporated Hawker Siddeley Aviation) and McDonnell Douglas.

A number of modifications were incorporated into the Harrier to suit US requirements and to improve the efficiency of the aircraft. The wing area was increased and the airfoil section was made thicker. Apart from improving the aerodynamic characteristics of the wing, the change in thickness made it possible to save weight. A thicker wing could have the same strength as a thin wing for less weight. The material of the wing structure was also changed from metal to

carbon-fibre-reinforced (graphite epoxy) composite. The height of the cockpit canopy was increased to accommodate more flight instrumentation and to improve the outward view for the pilot. All of these modifications were designed by McDonnell Douglas.

British Aerospace construct the centre and rear sections of the fuselage. These include the fin and rudder and the associated systems. On the present developed versions of the Harrier the tailplane is made of carbon-fibre composite material. This is made also by British Aerospace.

The front fuselage and the wings are made by McDonnell Douglas. In both cases the material is now carbon-fibre-reinforced (graphite/epoxy) composite.

The size of the wing has also been increased and a new aerodynamic section has been used to give more lift and enable

bigger payloads to be carried. The wing span of the AV-8B is 9.25m (30ft 4in) compared with 7.7m (25ft 3in) on the earlier versions. The increased wing size has allowed larger fuel tanks to be included inside the wing box. As a result, an extra 907kg (2,000lb) of fuel can be carried relative to earlier versions. This obviously has an important effect on the range of the aircraft.

The size of the flaps and ailerons has been increased too to make them more effective at low speed just after take-off. They also are now made of carbon-fibre-reinforced plastic material.

Other aerodynamic improvements include strakes running fore and aft underneath the weapons pod below the fuselage. These strakes are similar to shallow fins and their purpose is to prevent the exhaust jets from the engines being re-ingested back into the engine air intakes and to provide more lift during vertical take-offs. As was explained earlier, the engine performance would be adversely affected by the ingestion of hot exhaust gases.

The two downwards jets (one on each side of the aircraft) spread out sideways in all directions as they hit the ground. On

Right: The green/grey camouflage of the AV-8B well matches the aircraft's low-level, close air support mission. Also seen in this view is the Harrier II's improved visibility cockpit canopy, along with the repositioned outrigger housings which have been brought further inboard.

Opposite: This underside view of a Harrier II shows the large strakes runnning along below the fuselage. These help to prevent the hot exhaust gases from being sucked back into the engine intakes during vertical take-off and landing.

The TAV-8B Harrier II, a two-seat operational trainer version of the US Marine Corps' AV-8B.

the centreline of the aircraft they collide and are forced to turn back upwards. This upward stream of air hits the bottom of the fuselage. The strakes trap this air and make it exert a bigger upward force on the underside of the fuselage. This produces more lift during the take-off. The Harrier II also has the leading edge at the root of the wings extended to improve its rate of turn in combat conditions.

The dimensions and capabilities of the different versions of the Harrier at present in service are summarized on page 45 opposite, in a table of information provided by British Aerospace.

Although the Harrier is designed to operate with only one crew member, versions are available with two seats for training purposes. These aircraft carry all the armaments of the single-seater version and, therefore, can be used as active elements of the fighting services in time of war.

Harriers can be fitted with refuelling probes so that their range can be extended almost indefinitely by taking on fuel in flight from tanker aircraft. An idea of the development which has gone on in this sphere can be gained from the amazing fact that the furthest distance flown by a Harrier in one continuous hop is 7,403km (4,600 miles). The three Harriers involved were being delivered from McDonnell Douglas in St. Louis, Missouri, to the base of the Spanish Navy at Rota in the south of Spain. The total flight time was 9 hours

10 minutes. The KC-10 Extender tanker aircraft of the US Air Force refuelled each of the three aircraft in turn during the flight by means of the standard trailing drogue.

The Harrier has already proved so useful both in combat and in training exercises that its story is obviously just beginning. So far it has only seen action once in the Falklands campaign, where its contribution was decisive in securing a successful conclusion to the war. It is to be hoped that there will never again be the necessity to use it in anger. If such an occasion should occur, however, there is no doubt that even further refined versions of the Harrier will play a vital role in the defence of the Western alliance.

Particulars	Harrier GR3	Sea Harrier	Harrier II
	Metric/Imperial	Metric/Imperial	Metric/Imperial
Wing span	7.7m/25ft 3in	7.7m/25ft 3in	9.25m/30ft 4in
Overall length	14.27m/46ft 10in	14.5m/47ft 7in	14.12m/46ft 4in
Height	3.63m/11ft 11in	3.7m/12ft 2in	3.6m/11ft 8in
Wing area	18.7sq m/201sq ft	18.7sq m/201sq ft	21.4sq m/230sq ft
Wheel track	6.7m/22ft	6.7m/22ft	5.2m/17ft
Max. take-off weight	11,430kg/25,200lb	11,884kg/26,200lb	14,061kg/31,000lb
Operating weight empty	6,139kg/13,535lb	5,897kg/13,000lb	5,897kg/13,100lb
Max. warload	3,629kg/8,000lb	3,856kg/8,500lb	4,173kg/9,200lb
Internal fuel	2,295kg/5,060lb	2,295kg/5,060lb	3,520kg/7,760lb
Max. external fuel	2,404kg/5,300lb	2,404kg/5,300lb	3,629kg/8,000lb
First flight	August 1966	August 1978	April 1985
Power plant	Pegasus 103	Pegasus 104	Pegasus 105
Engine thrust	9,752kg/21,500lb	9,752kg/21,500lb	9,843kg/21,700lb
"g" limits	+7.8/−4.2	+7.8/−4.2	+7/−2.8
Max. speed: Sea level Dive speed	635kt Mach 1.3	635kt Mach 1.3	590kt Mach 1.1
Maximum payload for vertical take-off	2,268kg/5,000lb	2,268kg/5,000lb	3,062kg/6,750lb
Shortest take-off distance at max. take-off weight	304.8m/1,000ft	304.8m/1,000ft	305.5m/1,150ft

Index

Figures in italics refer to captions